Freedom
from
Shame

Find Healing for Your Most Toxic Emotion

GREGORY L. JANTZ, PHD
WITH KEITH WALL

AspirePress

Freedom from Shame: Find Healing for Your Most Toxic Emotion
© 2022 Gregory L. Jantz
Published by Aspire Press
An imprint of Tyndale House Ministries
Carol Stream, Illinois
www.hendricksonrose.com

ISBN 978-1-64938-047-0

Printed in the United States of America
010422VP

Contents

Why Shame Is *the* Most Toxic Emotion

"Shame on you!"

"You should be ashamed of yourself!"

"I'm so ashamed of you."

Have you heard phrases like these aimed at you? If so, you know how stinging and devastating the words are, leaving you feeling awful about yourself.

Even if you haven't heard caustic phrases like these hurled at you, it's likely you have felt the shame-on-you message through another person's veiled comments, nonverbal communication, silent treatment, or not-so-subtle actions.

Maybe it's been a long time since someone caused you to feel shamed, but now you carry feelings of being defective, unworthy, and inferior. You never feel at peace with yourself. You chronically feel disappointed with who you are. You question whether you're ever good enough. You compare yourself unfavorably to others. And you find yourself with self-condemning thoughts streaming through your mind:

- "How could I be so stupid?"

- "I always blow it when I need to step up!"

- "Dad was right. I'll never amount to anything."

I believe all people live with a life script, a distinct way they view themselves, their place in the world, how others regard them, and the way their life should unfold. Shame, pessimism, and low self-esteem dramatically inform your life script, almost always compromising relationship harmony, personal achievement, spiritual fulfillment, and daily joyful living.

So let me ask you: What is your life script? Do you see yourself as simply another cog in the overwhelming machine of random existence, or do you view yourself as someone of great value? What do you believe about God, yourself, and your place in the world? What caused a negative image of yourself?

As for me, I remember being terrified by math classes during my junior high and high school years. I can still hear two of my teachers telling me, "Gregg, you are just no good at math. You won't make it. Better choose a career that does not involve math."

That hurt! And the pain continued for years. Comments by two authority figures shaped my image of myself. Even in college, I almost didn't enter the field of psychology because I knew I'd have to take statistics.

Then one day, the tutor I'd hired to help me with my college math class said I could do it; I didn't need a tutor, and I could handle the class just fine on my own.

Wow, what a relief—and he was right. From that point on, I began to do well in math-related studies. But it was a long, painful wait before I found the courage and perseverance to do so.

My distorted self-image and sense of shame at being "no good" caused significant self-doubt and nearly derailed my career ambitions.

Think back on your own past experiences. What do you remember that may have blocked you from feeling good about yourself? Perhaps it was disparaging remarks by a teacher, parent, pastor, coach, or friend. Were you mistreated in ways that caused you to question your worth as a person? Shaming messages and behaviors are delivered in many ways, by various people, but they always result in a distorted sense of self and what it means to be loved and respected by others.

Time and again, as I have worked with people weighed down by shame and its consequences, I have been reminded of three essential points vital for you to know:

1. Shame is to the soul what cancer is to the body.

Scripture tells us that shame has been a part of the human condition from the very beginning. When Adam and Eve disobeyed God's instructions, they experienced shame and tried to hide: "Then the man and his wife heard the sound of the LORD God as he was walking in the garden in the cool of the day, and they hid from the LORD God among the trees of the garden" (Genesis 3:8). What was true then is true now: Shame causes us to hide our true selves—from God and from each other. Shame puts a stranglehold on both our emotional life and our spiritual life.

2. While God wants his children to experience freedom and fullness, shame keeps people trapped and troubled.

As a person of faith, I am convinced that God wants each person to be fulfilled, enjoy rewarding relationships, and grow into their full potential. Shame can plummet you into despair. But you don't need to stay there! As Scripture assures us, "It is for freedom that Christ has set us free. Stand firm, then, and do not let yourselves be burdened again by a yoke of slavery" (Galatians 5:1).

3. Freedom is possible for everyone, no matter how burdened they feel.

Although there are no quick fixes or magic formulas to cure our deepest pain, wellness and peace can be achieved based on reliable psychological principles, spiritual guidance, and dedicated effort. In the pages ahead, we'll explore the roots of shame, the damage it causes, and most importantly, the steps you can take to climb out of the pit of shame and onto the solid ground of wholeness and wellness.

Here's my promise: You can do hard things, and you're not alone. Right now, countless other people have embarked on the same journey. People just like you are shedding their shame, one moment, one day, one step at a time. By taking steps toward freedom, you will achieve the wholeness God intends for you—and the sense of worth you deserve!

CHAPTER 1

The Roots, Shoots, *and* Fruits *of* Shame

Morgan sat in the chair directly across from mine. As she gazed out the office window overlooking the ocean, I noticed how tired she appeared. The dark circles under her eyes were a deep shade of purple. I wondered if she had pulled an all-nighter at her office again—a habit we were working hard to break in our weekly sessions.

Morgan had sat in this exact seat every Monday without fail for the past six months, and most sessions started the same way. She would say, "I felt really unmotivated at work this week." She usually went on to tell me about her sixty-hour-per-week work schedule, the barrage of deadlines, and the seemingly endless meetings.

It always struck me that Morgan didn't so much share as she confessed. In Morgan's world, accomplishment was king. She was raised by two highly educated parents who were celebrated in their fields. Morgan's two older sisters followed suit, each excelling in high-profile careers. By all accounts, Morgan's apple had not fallen far from the tree. At barely twenty-five years old, her list of accomplishments was already a mile long. Gain admission into her college of choice: check. Graduate early and with honors: check. Earn a spot in a prestigious graduate program: check. Land a coveted, well-paying position straight out of school: check.

Despite her accolades and achievements, Morgan's view of herself remained static. Each week, she described herself using the same three words: unmotivated, irresponsible, and undeserving.

One week, I decided not to fill the silence with questions or affirmations. After several moments, Morgan sighed heavily, leaned forward, and rested her forehead in her hands. Tears fell softly onto the carpet. "I'm so tired of not being good enough," she said.

Morgan isn't alone in that feeling. Over the past three decades, I've counseled countless people who feel like they'll never measure up—people from all walks of life. Without fail, the story begins with "I'm not doing enough" and ends with "I'll never be enough."

There's a word for this feeling: *shame*.

Eventually, Morgan realized that she was, in fact, a highly motivated person. The problem was that she was motivated by the wrong thing.

Morgan described her upbringing as "stable and normal" and her parents as "loving but distant." She felt most connected to her parents when they expressed pride in her academic achievements. When Morgan fell behind in other areas of her life (like chores), her mother sometimes verbally lashed out, calling Morgan "lazy" and "ungrateful." Her father's response was more subtle, but no less painful. He simply gave her the silent treatment.

Morgan revealed that this caused her so much emotional pain that she learned to do everything in her power to avoid invoking her parents' disapproval. This resulted in changed behavior: Morgan's bedroom remained clean most of the time and she almost never forgot to empty the dishwasher.

As an adult, Morgan found that her own inner voice had taken on the same disapproving tone as her mother's. Instead of feeling motivated to work harder and get more done, however, Morgan felt too physically and mentally exhausted to maintain the backbreaking pace of life.

After meeting with Morgan for seven months, one Monday morning she walked into my office, took her usual seat, and shared that she hadn't gone to work for several days. She hadn't called in to report her absence either. She simply stopped showing up.

"I guess I really am a screw-up," she said.

■ ■ ■

Where Shame Starts

Shame has various root causes. Sometimes shame is instilled in early childhood by the harsh words or actions of parents or other authority figures, or from bullying by peers. Shame can stem from a person's own poor choices or harmful behavior. Other times unfortunate circumstances—such as poverty or chronic physical illness—plant seeds of shame. However, shame is much more than an uncomfortable feeling or a response to a humiliating event. Shame is a toxic emotion that drives an array of unhealthy attitudes and actions.

Psychologist Mary Lamia says this:

> Shame is a clear signal that our positive feelings have been interrupted. Another person or a circumstance can trigger shame in us, but so can a failure to meet our own ideals or standards. Given that shame can lead us to feel as though our whole self is flawed, bad, or subject to exclusion,

it motivates us to hide or to do something to save face. So it is no wonder that shame avoidance can lead to withdrawal or to addictions that attempt to mask its impact.[1]

SHAME IS A TOXIC EMOTION THAT DRIVES AN ARRAY OF UNHEALTHY ATTITUDES AND ACTIONS.

Though shame can begin in multiple ways, research studies and an accumulation of personal stories have revealed several prevalent sources.

Toxic Parents

Recently, a social media post that I found insightful made the rounds. The post read, "Be careful how you speak to your children, for your words become their inner voice." This one sentence managed to concisely summarize what child psychologists have been saying for years. Parents who joyfully and consistently attune to their children send the message that these young ones are worthy of connection. Children in these families trust that they can advocate for their emotional, social, and physical needs, and those needs are likely to be met. Over time, these children grow into adults who are sure of their own worth.

It would be wonderful if every child had such an upbringing. The reality is, the world is both broken and beautiful, and this is on full display in the home. Most parents try their best to love, nurture, and support their children. But sometimes, those efforts fall short of supplying children with what they need to develop lifelong self-esteem. And although the effects of emotional malnourishment are harder to spot, they are just as real and long-lasting as the physical kind.

> "SEE WHAT GREAT LOVE THE FATHER HAS LAVISHED ON US, THAT WE SHOULD BE CALLED CHILDREN OF GOD! AND THAT IS WHAT WE ARE!"
>
> –1 John 3:1

Perhaps the most destructive mistake parents make is conflating a child's actions with her character; equating what a child *does* with who she *is*. Recently, a client of mine, Tammy, shared a story about a time when she lied to her father. When she was ten, Tammy wanted to play outside with her younger brother instead of finishing her homework. "My dad asked if I was done with my math assignment, and I said yes," Tammy explained. "The next day, my teacher sent home a note to my parents to let them know I hadn't turned in the assignment. I'll never forget the look on Dad's face when he read that note. He looked at me with contempt. Disdain. I had never seen that look in his eyes. In that moment, I felt like a worm."

From then on, Tammy's father sometimes accused her of being a liar. In counseling, she expressed despair at having spent the following years trying to prove to him that she was an honest person. At some point, Tammy began to question all her other attributes. Was she really kind and generous? Was she truly capable and competent? The look on her father's face communicated that Tammy was repulsive; the label of *liar* stayed with her for decades. This became shame's song and the soundtrack of Tammy's life.

THIS IS AT THE HEART OF SHAME: THE BELIEF THAT YOU AND YOUR SIN ARE INDISTINGUISHABLE.

Of course, we all know that Tammy should not have lied to her father. The odds are good that Tammy's father was a well-intentioned man. If he had known that his words would emotionally scar his daughter, he would almost certainly yearn to take them back.

Tammy sinned by lying about her homework. But Tammy was first and foremost a child of God. Her earthly father made the mistake of identifying her with her sin. This is at the heart of shame: the belief that you and your sin are indistinguishable.

Abandonment or Rejection

People are wired for connection. We need genuine community. So what happens when an interpersonal connection is severed?

People experience abandonment and rejection for countless reasons. Families are torn apart by divorce, death, war, immigration, and deployment. Children perceive any loss as personal, no matter the cause. This belief has tragic consequences. It's common for children to take responsibility for their parents' divorce by thinking things like, *If only I had been better behaved, Dad would have stayed with Mom.*

SHAME CAUSES US TO PULL AWAY FROM RELATIONSHIPS, BELIEVING THAT WE ARE BAD FOR OTHER PEOPLE AND UNWORTHY OF THEIR LOVE.

Such a burden is far too heavy for a young person to shoulder. By the time this child reaches adulthood, he will be accustomed to accepting responsibility for events he has no control over. If we didn't shoulder the blame for our own abandonment, we might have to place the burden squarely on the shoulders of someone we dearly love—and that is often harder than incurring the blame ourselves.

Shame causes us to pull away from relationships, believing that we are bad for other people and unworthy of their love. Ironically, the experience of being abandoned often leads people to self-imposed exile.

In the chapters ahead, we'll look at steps you can take to move out of this kind of isolation and into healthy relationships with others.

Unhealthy Environments

Every workplace, organization, group, and team has a distinct culture that develops over time. This is characterized by the way people interact, the energy displayed when people are together, the respect or disrespect shown to each other, the camaraderie or hostility, and many other factors. One description by business leaders explains:

> Organizational culture refers to a system of shared assumptions, values, and beliefs that show people what is appropriate and inappropriate behavior. These values have a strong influence on employee behavior as well as organizational performance.... Culture is largely invisible to individuals just as the sea is invisible to the fish swimming in it.[2]

An unhealthy work environment can be shame-inducing because employees begin to wonder what they've done to deserve such treatment—and worry that they're unimportant. Worse, bosses sometimes use shame, manipulation, and passive-aggressive tactics, which may motivate employees in the short term but ultimately leave them demoralized.

The workplace is just one example. A school can be an inspiring place to learn or a viper's nest of bullying. Churches can be life-giving or legalistic. Sports teams can be encouraging or critical. Peer groups can be supportive or distressing. Even something as simple as a book group can have one domineering know-it-all member who makes others feel small when they share the "wrong" opinion.

WE ARE DEEPLY INFLUENCED BY THE PEOPLE WE SPEND TIME WITH.

We are deeply influenced by the people we spend time with. When we feel that we matter, we develop a strong sense of identity. But when we feel unimportant or burdensome to others, we naturally take responsibility and internalize shame.

Setting sturdy boundaries and dealing with offenses in such environments are some of the ways you can safeguard yourself from this shame. We'll discuss steps how to do this effectively in the pages ahead.

Unhealthy Religious Leaders

Religion can enhance our individual lives, strengthen marriages, and fortify families. Religious communities can bring people together and mobilize them to serve locally and beyond. There is nothing so powerful as a healthy church, guided by humble people who lead by example. It makes sense, then, that institutions that have the potential to be agents of healing also have the potential to be agents of pain. In fact, one of the most potent sources of shame comes from within our sacred spaces.

I believe that most religious leaders are people of integrity and honesty, striving to be models of service and love. But sadly this is not always the case, as some misuse their positions of power. In such situations, the worst part is that this pain is experienced as disapproval, not just from human leaders and other members of the congregation, but also from God. This type of shame can be one of the hardest to heal. It causes people to doubt the love of the very One who would heal and restore them.

The Bible is clear that nothing and no one—not even powerful religious leaders—can separate us from the love of God in Christ:

> Who will bring any charge against those whom God has chosen? It is God who justifies. Who then is the one who condemns? No one.… Who shall separate us from the love of Christ? Shall trouble or hardship or persecution or famine or nakedness or danger or sword?... No, in all these things we are more than conquerors through him who loved us. (Romans 8:33–37)

Traumatic Experiences

Trauma is any experience that overwhelms the brain's ability to cope. Young children require constant attention and care, in part because they are physically helpless and psychologically vulnerable. When something overwhelms a child's ability to cope, she needs a safe adult to come alongside her and help her feel secure again.

Children grow into resilient adults when they face hardship with the support of a caring adult. Without such a caregiver, a child who faces an overwhelming experience can feel powerless and ashamed. He may believe that these circumstances befell him because he was fundamentally flawed and unworthy of goodness. Sadly, childhood abuse often leaves survivors feeling irreparably marred, leading to thoughts such as:

- "Mom drank because I was such a disappointment to her. I'm still disappointing the people I love."

- "I should have been able to protect my sister from danger, and her death was my fault. Everything is my fault now."

I have heard stories like these countless times in my work with clients, and each one is heartbreaking. When it comes to trauma, the initial event is often harrowing, but the lingering shame is most devastating. But as with other sources of shame, we can be free from trauma-induced shame as we learn to replace the false perceptions we had as children with a true picture and understanding of the painful experiences in our past.

Personal or Moral Failures

I've listened to many clients who believe they deserve to feel shame due to their own indiscretions and moral failings. These people are locked inside a prison of their own making, and shame is the warden. They live as though shame's constant reminders will ensure that they don't make the same mistake twice.

It can be difficult to help these people heal from shame because shame serves a function in their lives while at the same time causing them misery. Self-compassion is key for these people, and it is possible to foster self-compassion while also accepting responsibility for what you've done.

I will never forget a client, Bob, who had cheated on his wife. Once she found out, the couple began marriage counseling. Bob was tremendously remorseful and assured his wife that the affair had nothing to do with her. Instead, he realized that he had unmet and unexpressed longings—longings that weren't exclusively sexual in nature. He wanted to feel important and interesting to someone else, and he was attracted to a woman who made him feel those things.

For a brief time, Bob felt on top of the world. But after the affair was exposed, his self-esteem plummeted back down to earth. If he felt unimportant and boring previously, he felt even worse now. His new label of *cheater* only compounded his already low self-concept.

His wife, still reeling with pain herself, saw no problem with her husband's shame. In fact, they both embraced shame almost like a third party in the marriage. They both needed to see that shame was not the same as remorse, and compassion didn't mean letting Bob off the hook for his behavior.

IT IS POSSIBLE TO FOSTER SELF-COMPASSION WHILE ALSO ACCEPTING RESPONSIBILITY FOR WHAT YOU'VE DONE.

Eventually, they came to view shame as a wedge between them. They began to experience real change when they replaced shame with compassion and understanding.

GUILT VS. SHAME

Many people lump shame and guilt together in the same cauldron of toxic emotions. But there are important distinctions, and understanding them will help you move beyond shame.

Guilt

- Guilt refers to our sense of having done something wrong, either in reality or in our imagination.

- Guilt relates to actions or inactions that have caused real or imagined harm to others.

- Guilt can lead to a sense of having to pay a debt or repair something.

- Psychologists, as well as religious teachers, usually view guilt as a corrective response—that is, this emotion alerts us to an error or misdeed we've committed that needs to be remedied.

Shame

- Shame relates to our sense of who we are.

- With shame, we feel that we have fallen short in our own eyes, in the eyes of others, and in the eyes of God.

- Shame causes us to feel a need to hide or conceal an aspect of ourselves. In fact, the word *shame* derives from the Indo-European word *skem*, which means "to cover."

Guilt and shame often go hand in hand. We might feel guilty about something we have done but ashamed about how this reflects on who we are. Guilt is often overt and up front, whereas shame tends to hide itself and is often harder to identify.

In short, guilt involves something we have done, while shame involves who we are.

GUILT SAYS, "YOU FAILED."

SHAME SAYS, "YOU'RE A FAILURE."

GRACE SAYS, "YOUR FAILURES ARE FORGIVEN."

—Lecrae

Shame *and* Your Health

We've all laid awake in bed at night, replaying scenarios in our head. We think about things we could've done differently—what we should have said, how life might be better—if we had only put our best foot forward. As our stress levels rise, so does the shame we experience. That can keep a person tossing and turning all night, sometimes for years on end.

Our bodies require sleep to process our experiences and to support our immune system. Shame-induced insomnia is only one of the ways our bodies pay the price for our shame. We can find ourselves in a vicious cycle: health issues stemming from shame can undermine work performance and relational satisfaction, which in turn give way to more shame. In this way, shame can have a real impact on your physical health.

Susceptibility to Addiction and Other Mental Health Issues

Over the past fifty years, scientists and researchers have made great strides in understanding the complexities of mental health issues. We now know that while behavior modification can alleviate some mental problems, such as anxiety and depression, oftentimes a more in depth solution is needed.

While the remedies for addictions such as alcoholism, gambling, overeating, or sex aren't the same, there are common factors. And while it is not within the scope of this short book to thoroughly analyze the complexities of addiction, it's important to bring up a few key factors:

- In my work as a mental health professional, I have never met an addict who didn't struggle with shame. You can medicate and psychoanalyze an individual, and brief breakthroughs may occur, but they rarely last if shame is still present.

- While addiction typically has a biochemical root, the road toward addiction is accelerated by the wounds shame brings.

- Breaking free from mental illness and addiction often involves a multipronged approach involving spiritual renewal (breaking the bondage of the shame cycle), healthy emotional and mental habits, and (especially with severe depression and anxiety) medication.

It's critical to remember that the most incendiary fuel for the firestorm of mental illness and addiction is shame. Understanding that fact—that shame is an enemy that must be defeated—is critical for breaking free from mental health issues or addiction.

Body Shaming

Among the many varieties of shaming, in recent decades body shaming (also known as fat shaming) has become one of the most common—and most damaging.

Body shaming occurs when individuals are judged negatively based on their physical appearance and ridiculed for it. Generally, men and women are fat shamed if they appear overweight or don't fit the idyllic image of thin and beautiful. However, researchers note that thin shaming is also a negative form of judgment and bullying as well.

According to the *Oxford English Dictionary*, body shaming is defined as "the action or practice of mocking or stigmatizing someone by making critical comments about the shape, size, or appearance of their body."[3]

Psychologists and researchers specializing in media effects on the body and mind agree that body shaming has likely always been a problem in modern society to a degree. However, with the advent of the Internet and social media platforms, public commentary on all matters is at an all-time high, including bullying and shaming individuals for their weight and appearance.

THE MOST INCENDIARY FUEL FOR THE FIRESTORM OF MENTAL ILLNESS AND ADDICTION IS SHAME.

Consider this:

- 94 percent of teenage girls have been body shamed.[4]

- Nearly 65 percent of teen boys reported having been body shamed.[5]

- Approximately 91 percent of women are unhappy with their bodies. Only 5 percent of women naturally possess the body type portrayed as ideal by American media.[6]

Body shaming creates a range of problems for targeted individuals: diminished self-esteem, distorted body image, and elevated risk of eating disorders. Research has demonstrated that those with a poor body image—often a result of body shaming—have an increased risk of heart and metabolic diseases.[7]

While obesity brings its own health risks to an individual, body shaming can be just as detrimental, especially among impressionable teens and adolescents who struggle with self-esteem and confidence.

Social Media

Social media can be a powerful tool to reinforce shame. Social media users may believe that in order to be relevant or to "influence," they need to craft an image of themselves that is interesting and unique. Not only that, but they need to be *more* interesting and unique than the next person. For instance, if you can't seem to grow a following or your photo doesn't get as many "likes" as someone else's, it's easy to feel as though there must be something wrong with you. And if you post something on social media that violates a social norm (intentionally or otherwise), you're at risk of public humiliation.

IF COMPARISON IS THE THIEF OF JOY, THEN SOCIAL MEDIA IS DRIVING THE GETAWAY CAR.

What's more, social media can induce shame when we take online content at face value. It's easy to forget that the photo shoot was staged, the images were Photoshopped, and the content was cleverly crafted. We can fall victim to feeling like our life is lackluster compared to what we see online. If comparison is the thief of joy, then social media is driving the getaway car.

The risks to your emotional health are real. In one study, the World Health Organization found that:

> Excessive use of the Internet and electronic devises can be associated with a range of social and psychological problems, such as poor psychological wellbeing, poor self-confidence, family problems, marital breakdown, and reduced work and academic performance.[8]

In fact, a growing body of research in recent years has found that while social media can have some benefits to users, for many people the risks of harm to their psychological wellbeing are significant.

Defeating *the* Enemy

Shame is an enemy that must be dealt with head on. It won't go away by avoiding it. Hiding from shame with procrastination or trying to outrun it with "driving and striving" will not bring freedom from its stranglehold on your life. It must be defeated.

For some people who struggle with shame, attempting to do even small projects seems daunting. Even a simple task can feel out of reach. So they put it off, bury their heads in the sand, afraid to face the day. This procrastination just reinforces the negative beliefs of shame. Whether consciously or subconsciously, they think: *Well, if I don't try, I can't fail.* A person who feels constant shame might believe: *If I were a better person or had a stronger work ethic, I would have started this project ages ago and the final product would be so much better.* This person lives in the shadow of the person they wish they could be.

Shame can also compel people to frantically and constantly do more and achieve more as a way to try to prove they are worthy of respect and admiration.

These people "drive and strive" to overcompensate for their feelings of shame. They run the risk of becoming workaholics, obsessed with accumulating a resumé of awards and triumphs.

> "FOR YOU CREATED MY INMOST BEING; YOU KNIT ME TOGETHER IN MY MOTHER'S WOMB. I PRAISE YOU BECAUSE I AM FEARFULLY AND WONDERFULLY MADE."
>
> –Psalm 139:13-14

There's certainly nothing wrong with pursuing goals and accomplishing ambitions. But external achievements will never heal the pain of shame and help us grow into the people we're intended to become—children of God free from shame and secure in his love!

When we have internal wounds that are painful to face, the easiest thing to do is avoid them and fill our heads and days with "the tyranny of the urgent." The problem is those negative emotions—such as shame—just sit there in the background. This means shame has been covered over or pushed to the side by busyness—but it hasn't been dealt with. It's lurking in the shadows, waiting to reappear when the frenetic activity stops.

If you struggle in these areas, stop trying to hide from your shame or outrun your troubles by outperforming your competitors. Neither will lead to the kind of peace Jesus spoke of: "Peace I leave with you; my peace I give you. I do not give to you as the world gives. Do not let your hearts be troubled and do not be afraid" (John 14:27).

■ ■ ■

I began this chapter by telling you about my client Morgan, whose shame drove her to try to prove herself by chasing one accomplishment after another—which eventually caused her to burn out and give up. Her road hasn't been a smooth one, but Morgan came to see shame as a part of herself that was crowding out all of her other inner parts. Shame was taking up so much mental and emotional space that she no longer had room to be creative, playful, or spontaneous.

One afternoon, Morgan mused aloud, "I wonder how much I have missed out on because I was so busy trying to appease my shame?" That question was a turning point, as she began to see herself and her shame as separate entities. Who she is as a person is different from what she does.

Most of all, Morgan is learning to view herself as a much-loved child of God. She's replacing the messages of shame with thoughts of truth. "I'm unmotivated and lazy" has been replaced by "I don't need to strive to be good enough; God has already declared me worthy." The more this truth sinks in and the more she practices replacing old scripts with new ones, the more grace she is able to extend to herself.

How much has shame taken from you over the years? What has it cost you in terms of relationships, job opportunities, and adventures? If shame has ruled your life for too long and you're ready to take a step onto a new path, you're not alone. You are pursuing freedom and fulfillment along with many other people on this journey with you.

Unaddressed shame can lead to so many harmful consequences in your life. The good news is that toxic spills and waste sites can be cleaned up! Next, let's explore ways to achieve a shame-free life.

CHAPTER 2

Replacing *the* Script *of* Shame

Samuel grew up in war-torn Somalia. As a child his family was caught in the middle of a firefight between rebels and government forces. Both of his parents were killed and his older brother, Wisdom, was left with an inoperable bullet in his back, paralyzing him.

The two boys were adopted by an aunt and raised on the outskirts of Mogadishu. Samuel is now twenty and cares for Wisdom and does what he can scavenging car parts from a local auto dump to sell in the marketplace. His aunt is ill and can't work full time, and his uncle has been in another part of the country trying to find work.

Samuel carries a heavy load, made heavier by the fact that he feels that no matter how hard he tries, it's never good enough. There is never enough food, and he feels shame that he can't afford the medicine Wisdom deserves. Though Samuel strives to serve God, he senses that he has let God down. No matter what he does, he feels like God is still disappointed in him. Samuel longs to be accepted by God but never feels like he can bring in enough income or food to please God or his family.

ONE WAY TO SUSTAIN OPTIMISM, HOPE, AND JOY IS TO INTENTIONALLY FILL OUR THOUGHTS WITH POSITIVE SELF-TALK.

Halfway around the world, Julia lives in a suburb outside Vancouver, British Columbia. She and Philip, her husband of eleven years, have two young daughters. The economically secure couple run an import business together and have done well for themselves. They met at a church camp in college and married immediately after graduation. Julia is an earnest person—dependable, conscientious, and always looking for ways to help her husband and daughters.

Julia can't remember the last time she didn't feel exhausted emotionally or physically. At a recent lunch with a girlfriend, she described her current state as spiritually anorexic. No matter how much she tries to feel God's love, the sense of his grace is outweighed by the shame she feels for her failures as a mom and wife. She told her friend, "I feel like I'm wasting away and the only emotions I experience any more are anger, guilt, and shame."

Samuel's and Julia's lives are so radically different that they might as well be living on different planets. However, the one thing they both have in common is that they believe their best efforts are never "good enough"—for themselves, for their families, for God. This belief is their "script" and it's one that many people struggling with shame find very familiar.

In this chapter, we'll discuss ways to overwrite the false script of shame with the voice of truth and freedom.

■ ■ ■

Tap *the* Power *of* Positive Self-Talk

Each of us has a set of messages that replay in our minds. This internal dialogue or personal commentary frames our reactions to life and its circumstances. One way to sustain optimism, hope, and joy is to intentionally fill our thoughts with positive self-talk.

Too often, the pattern of self-talk we've developed is negative. We remember the unconstructive things we were told as children by our parents, siblings, or teachers. We remember the negative reactions from other children that diminished how we felt about ourselves. Throughout the years, these messages have replayed in our minds, fueling anger, fear, guilt, and hopelessness.

One of the most important techniques we use in therapy with those struggling with shame is to identify the source of these messages and then work with the person to intentionally overwrite them. If a person learned as a child that he was worthless, we show him how truly special he is. If a person learned while growing up to expect crises and destructive events, we show her a better way to anticipate the future.

Try the following exercise. Write down some of the negative messages inside your mind that undermine your ability to overcome your shame. Be specific, whenever possible, and include anyone you remember who contributed to that message.

Now, take a moment to intentionally counteract those negative messages with positive truths in your life. Don't give up if you don't find them quickly. For every negative message there is a positive truth that will override the weight of shame. These truths always exist; keep looking until you find them.

POSITIVE SELF-TALK IS ABOUT RECOGNIZING THE TRUTH, IN SITUATIONS AND IN YOURSELF.

You may have a negative message that replays in your head every time you make a mistake. As a child you were told:

- "You're worthless."

- "Why can't you ever do anything right?"

When you make a mistake, you can choose to overwrite that message with a positive one, such as:

- "I make mistakes sometimes, just like everyone. All it means is that I'm human."

- "I choose to accept and grow from my mistake."

- "As I learn from my mistakes, I am becoming a better person."

During this exercise, mistakes become opportunities to replace negative views of who you are with positive options for personal enhancement.

Positive self-talk is not self-deception. It is not mentally looking at circumstances with eyes that see only what you want to see. Rather, positive self-talk is about recognizing the truth, in situations and in yourself. One of the fundamental realities is that you will make mistakes. To expect perfection in yourself or anyone else is unrealistic. To expect no difficulties in life, whether through your own actions or sheer circumstances, is also unreasonable.

When negative events or mistakes happen, positive self-talk seeks to bring the good out of the bad to help you do better, go further, or just keep moving forward.

THE NEGATIVE MESSAGE IS ...

OVERWRITE THE NEGATIVE MESSAGE WITH ...

THE NEGATIVE MESSAGE IS ...

OVERWRITE THE NEGATIVE MESSAGE WITH ...

THE NEGATIVE MESSAGE IS . . .

OVERWRITE THE NEGATIVE MESSAGE WITH . . .

THE NEGATIVE MESSAGE IS . . .

OVERWRITE THE NEGATIVE MESSAGE WITH . . .

Know *that* You Are Worthy

Shame-filled people feel unworthy even when good things happen to them or they achieve an important goal. As soon as they start to dream about something exciting and hopeful, it's closely followed by the belief that they don't deserve those good things. Even if they do achieve something they've worked hard for, their joy is robbed from them by the "impostor syndrome"—they doubt themselves and feel like a phony. For people plagued by shame, the bar is always moving, and they often fall into despair, believing they will never arrive.

THE WAY TO COMBAT FEELINGS OF WORTHLESSNESS IS TO FOCUS ON THE TRUTHS OF WHO WE ARE AT OUR CORE.

Over and over in Scripture, God speaks his worth to us, his beloved children. But if we are convinced we're unworthy of love, we have difficulty receiving God's love.

Yet Scripture tells us that we are "fearfully and wonderfully made" (Psalm 139:14). Fearfully here means with great care, craft, and concern. In you, God crafted a one-of-a-kind masterpiece. Indeed, there is nothing more precious to him on this planet than one of his children.

The way to combat feelings of worthlessness is to focus on the truths of who we are at our core. Let's take a moment to list just a few of the qualities and traits that God attributes to his children:

- **We have been bought with a price, and we belong to God.**
  "Do you not know that your bodies are temples of the Holy Spirit, who is in you, whom you have received from God? You are not your own; you were bought at a price. Therefore honor God with your bodies" (1 Corinthians 6:19–20).

- **We have been chosen and appointed to bear fruit.**
  "You did not choose me, but I chose you and appointed you so that you might go and bear fruit—fruit that will last—and so that whatever you ask in my name the Father will give you" (John 15:16).

- **We are holy and blameless in his sight.**
  "For he chose us in him before the creation of the world to be holy and blameless in his sight" (Ephesians 1:4).

- **We are God's handiwork.**
  "For we are God's handiwork, created in Christ Jesus to do good works, which God prepared in advance for us to do" (Ephesians 2:10).

Worthless is not a word Scripture uses to describe us—ever. If God created us and loves us, then he values us. Don't let shame or your past trauma give you a false sense of your worth. At times we all doubt our worth, but God never does.

Replace *Your* Filters

For those struggling with shame, regret and disappointment can take permanent residence in the heart. It's understandable to have remorse, but it's also dangerous to remain stuck in our regrets and past. Feeling stuck or trapped is always linked to a lack of hope for present and future circumstances. Shame-filled people often have a pessimistic view of themselves and their future. They feel anchored to past failures and traumas. They believe they're unable to grow into the free and full individuals they long to be.

> "WHETHER YOU THINK YOU CAN OR YOU CAN'T, YOU'RE RIGHT."
>
> Henry Ford

Your feelings of shame are rooted in your view of who you are, how other people perceive you, and your place in relationships and the world. One way to think of these perceptions is as filters through which you view the events of your life. Some people, who seem perennially happy, are considered to view life through rose-colored glasses. Their filters are weighted on the side of the positive. For people struggling with shame, life is viewed through gray-colored glasses. Life appears negative, oppressive, and filled with shadows.

If you believe that life consistently treats you unfairly, then the inevitable ups and downs are filtered through that perception. Up-times seem imaginary and are enjoyed (if at all) with suspicion. Times of disappointment are considered normal or expected. Every down-time that happens strengthens the idea that it's just the way your life is. If you have the perception

that you don't really deserve to be happy, you will filter the events of your life to make sure you aren't content. If you have the perception that the only way for you to be safe is to be in control, you will have a heightened sense of anxiety about life events. Because people are rarely in total control over their environment, and never in control of other people, this perception leaves a persistent, nagging feeling of insecurity. This perpetual sense of unease can lead to anxiety and depression. Additionally, perceptions are so powerful that they can become engines for a self-fulfilling prophecy. What we *expect* to happen usually does.

By acknowledging negative perceptions, you can move forward toward a view of life that is neither unrealistically rosy nor unrelentingly gray. Acknowledging your script, patterns, and perceptions allows you to manage them, altering them to support your optimism, hope, and joy, even when life is difficult.

So how do you go about altering your perceptions and revising your life script? Start with these strategies:

Write it out.

Many of the people I work with find great freedom of expression through journaling. This activity has an added benefit of providing a record of thoughts, feelings, and events that you can refer to as your healing journey progresses. The key is to write as if no one will ever read your journal entries, so you can be completely open and honest without self-editing. Along with painful experiences brought on by shame, look for the positives in yourself, your life, and your expectations for the day or week ahead. This will set the stage for optimism, hope, and joy to make a daily appearance.

Talk it out with yourself.

Another way to reorient your attitude is to have a heart-to-heart conversation with yourself. Some people do this silently, inside their own minds. Others prefer to hold an audible conversation with themselves. One woman I worked with would argue with herself like an opposing attorney, talking to herself out loud. She said it helped to hear what she had to say audibly because she had an easier time detecting the emotions underlying the various topics. However you choose to have a dialogue with yourself, you'll find value in putting it into words and requiring yourself to think about the reasons behind your beliefs and actions.

What should you discuss with yourself? Here are a few discussion starters:

- When I feel shame bubbling to the surface, how do I typically respond? How would I like to respond differently in the future?

- Where did my shame come from originally? What has been my part in living out a life script influenced by shame?

- How have I let shame negatively direct my thoughts and actions? How can I turn these to the positive?

- Who am I now and who do I want to become?

Talk it out with a trusted counselor, friend, or mentor.

A biblical proverb says, "Plans fail for lack of counsel, but with many advisers they succeed" (Proverbs 15:22). Seek input and guidance from people whose judgment you trust. When you've finally chosen to address your shame and work through it, you might find yourself vulnerable and susceptible to missteps. We all have blind spots, and these are even more pronounced when our heart is raw and tender. That's why

> "PLANS FAIL FOR LACK OF COUNSEL, BUT WITH MANY ADVISERS THEY SUCCEED."
> —Proverbs 15:22

you need a counselor—a therapist, a close friend, or a trusted family member. Be open-minded as you ask, "How can I address the consequences of shame that are holding me back? What should I be doing differently?" A wise counselor can save you from further heartache— and cheer you on to wholeness and health.

Cultivate *an* Optimistic Outlook

No one needs to look far to find negativity. Cable news, social media, the workplace, and even our homes—it's there. Combining the negativity in the world around us with our inner struggles with shame can create a potent mix of toxicity in our soul. The result is that we begin to view our world through a critical lens, and instead of seeing what's positive around us, all we see is the negative.

Researchers have long understood that a person's attitude largely determines his or her success in a wide range of areas: career, athletics, financial goals, and relationships. If you are a pessimist by nature or because of the shame you have experienced, you can make changes and form habits that will shift your thinking from negative to positive. If you are already an optimist, you can become even more optimistic.

Wherever you currently stand on the optimist-pessimist continuum, here are some ways to boost your positive outlook:

- **Don't let tomorrow spoil today.** Worrying about tomorrow's troubles—which may or may not happen—steals your happiness in the present moment.

- **Affirm others often.** Be generous with your compliments. By helping others feel good about themselves, you'll feel better about yourself too.

- **Affirm yourself often.** Giving yourself compliments throughout the day will provide a boost to your self-confidence.

- **Learn from the past, but don't be anchored by it.** You can't change anything about your history, but you can influence your future by working through hurts that hold you back.

- **Pay attention to your thoughts.** You control what goes on in your mind. Steer those internal messages toward hopeful, positive expectations.

- **Realize that an optimistic outlook fosters opportunity.** Optimism is a self-fulfilling prophecy: Research has shown that people who consistently think positively create more opportunities for themselves.

- **Be mindful of what you say.** Your thoughts are like an arrow made of positive or negative intention. Words are the bow that fires them into the world, and they will land where you aim.

- **Practice healthy habits.** No one denies the link between physical and emotional well-being.

Regular exercise and good nutrition go a long way toward promoting a positive attitude.

- **Plan to play.** If your lifestyle does not include enough play, schedule time for recreation the way you would a meeting or an appointment.

- **Surround yourself with optimistic allies.** Optimism is contagious, so bring together your group of positive people.

With small, intentional decisions each day, you can change your outlook from negative to hopeful and promising.

Cover *Your* Wounds *with* Grace

Growing up, Martin was always overweight. Given today's healthcare parameters, he would've been categorized as obese. Other children were unbelievably cruel, and Martin remembers hating school because of the taunts, jokes, and isolation. His peers became his enemies, and he never really did get over that dynamic as an adult. The weight eventually came off, with concerted effort, but the defensive mindset stayed. Martin developed an aggressive approach to any perceived slight, determined to never feel targeted again.

Shame causes us to be hypersensitive to any perceived put-down and criticism. As we work through the aftermath of trauma or other painful events that caused shame, we often wear extremely thin skin. Any comment or action that has even the appearance of being hurtful is immediately interpreted as a personal attack. Why? Because we haven't fully healed yet.

GRACE IS THE BANDAGE THAT COVERS THE HURTS AND ALLOWS THEM TO HEAL.

We allow the comment or the action to touch that tender spot, and it hurts. Grace can help us with this—and we can seek to respond graciously to hurtful people. This doesn't mean you have to pretend that the wounds aren't still raw or partially healed. But you can shield those tender spots by allowing grace to cover them, deflecting what might yet be painful.

> "THE LORD LONGS TO BE GRACIOUS TO YOU; THEREFORE HE WILL RISE UP TO SHOW YOU COMPASSION."
>
> —Isaiah 30:18

Grace is the bandage that covers the hurts and allows them to heal. This means giving people the benefit of the doubt. When you're not absolutely sure that something was meant to harm you, assume it wasn't, and go on from there. If someone means to hurt you, it will become evident in time, and you can guard yourself or confront it when it does. (We'll discuss how to set protective boundaries in the next chapter.)

1. If a person says something you perceive as insulting, you might think: *Wow, that was mean.*

2. The nature of your thought then generates your emotional response: *What an insult! That really hurt!* Your perception becomes visceral in the form of a negative emotion.

Just as negative thoughts lead to negative emotions, positive thoughts lead to positive emotions and, by extension, better overall emotional health. In the example above, let's say you've committed to think the best of people instead of the worst.

1. When someone makes what could be interpreted as a mean remark, you choose to think instead: *Okay, this person is having a tough day.*

2. This way of perceiving the remark gives people the benefit of the doubt and removes meanness from the equation. Your emotional response is then more likely to be compassionate: *I'll ask him if there's anything I can do to help today.*

In Martin's case, his employer finally suggested he get counseling through the company's Employee Assistance Program. After a series of sessions, Martin was able to return to his painful childhood memories and extend grace to those long-ago bullies and tormentors. He learned to relax around his coworkers and give them the benefit of the doubt. Martin is happier now, and so is everyone around him.

Our lives, like Martin's, can be filled with casual cruelty. We would like to lash out and fight back. But the apostle Paul tells us, "Let your conversation be always full of grace, seasoned with salt, so that you may know how to answer everyone" (Colossians 4:6). Cushioned by grace, we are to respond with gentleness instead of anger. This implies intentionality, which is a primary component of grace.

CHAPTER 3

Learning *to* Believe *in* Yourself

In the Introduction, I told you about my struggles as a high schooler. As a junior, I was unmotivated, unsure of myself, and unclear about my future. I watched my GPA slide downward along with my self-esteem. Then, during the summer between my junior and senior years, I attended Victory Cove Camp in McCall, Idaho.

On the first day there, I met a counselor named John, who, for some reason, decided to take me under his wing and pour himself into my life. He invited me to sit at his table during mealtimes, telling stories about himself and asking about my life. During activities and competitions, he would often accompany me, offering encouraging words: "Great job, Gregg! Wow, you did amazing!" After chapel services, he would pull me aside to discuss what we had heard the speaker say, always with warmth and affirmation.

Like many people struggling with lack of confidence, I thought, *Why did John single me out for special treatment? He could have chosen to spend time with another kid with more talent and more potential than me.* Nevertheless, I felt honored and lifted up. In other words, I felt believed in.

On the last day of camp, a cross-country race was held for anyone who wanted to participate. Since I had never considered myself particularly athletic and had never run a distance race, I chose not to enter. But then John said, "You should do it, Gregg. I believe in you and think you'll do well. Besides, it's better to try than to sit on the sidelines wondering what might have happened."

Despite his nudging, I declined. I didn't want to embarrass myself with a lousy showing—or worse, not finishing the race. But then inspiration struck. At the very last minute, I sprinted to the starting line. If John believes I can do it, I reasoned, then maybe I can. At least I can try. At the end of that ten-mile race, I shocked myself, and many others, when I came in first place! John met me at the finish line with hugs and high-fives.

"I knew it!" he said. "I knew you had it in you!"

■ ■ ■

What Does It Mean *to* Believe *in* Yourself?

Shame-filled people have been conditioned to not believe in themselves. That's why the key word in this chapter is *learning*. You can take steps to move in the direction of affirming who you are as a whole person, with a combination of strengths and weaknesses, assets and liabilities—just like everyone on earth.

But what exactly does it mean to "believe in yourself"? It begins with accepting truths about yourself that are healthy and empowering, such as:

- ■ "I am more than my mistakes."

- ■ "I'm capable of learning what I need to learn."

- ■ "I have value—always."

- ■ "I am stronger than I think I am."

- ■ "I can make a positive difference in the lives of people around me."

These statements are powerful because they advocate believing something positive and true about yourself even if your circumstances or experiences could lead you to believe otherwise. When you affirm strong qualities about yourself, you're more likely to convince other people to believe the best about you too. To bolster your belief in yourself, consider these strategies:

- **Stop ruminating on past mistakes.** Make a list of things you can do to disrupt negative thoughts the next time you find yourself beating yourself up over blunders.

- **Continually learn new things.** Take a class. Read a book. Follow an instructional YouTube video. The more you master the art of learning, the more confidence you'll have in your ability to continue growing and gaining competence.

- **Take a risk.** Step outside your comfort zone and reach for something you want—and for a greater sense of empowerment. Start a blog, move to a new neighborhood, publish your poetry, audition for a play, ask for a raise, or get to know somebody new.

- **Love others.** Set a daily goal of making a positive difference in the life of someone you know or meet. Studies show that when you are kind to other people, it increases your own self-esteem and overall happiness.

- **Identify one issue and work through it.** All of us have a weakness or shortcoming that holds us back.

Think about one aspect you want to improve upon and go for it. Get help from books, podcasts, a counselor, or close friends.

- ■ **Engage with life in ways that leave you feeling empowered.** To begin with, spend less time by yourself on your phone and more time pursuing activities that are life-giving to you.

Accept Kindness *from* Others

As we have discussed, shame causes us to be guarded, wary of others' motives, and reluctant to receive compliments and acts of kindness, believing we aren't deserving. We're accustomed to being tricked, manipulated, and lied to. A big step in your healing, therefore, is the willingness to receive good things from good people.

Because the voice of shame is constantly accusing you of being unworthy, it can be incredibly difficult to believe that you deserve love and affection. Shame can lead us to pull away from safe people and instead seek companionship in the wrong places.

Oftentimes, shame leads to isolation. Time and again, clients have told me that their feelings of shame and regret have driven them away from others. In fact, one of the most destructive side effects of shame is loneliness. It's that feeling that no one else can relate to what we are going through, that our past has branded us an outcast. Shame-filled people need healthy, affirming people to mirror acceptance, grace, and genuine love.

When you encounter someone who genuinely wants to help you and who believes in you, keep in mind:

■ People who struggle with shame are often mistrustful of others—and that's understandable. Pause to think through if this person has given you any reason for doubt. If not, continue with a spirit of openness.

■ Express appreciation. If someone shows kindness to you, tell that person that you are grateful.

■ Write in your journal about your responses and feelings about a new person who is showing you kindness. Describing your thoughts in writing will help clarify your aspects of concern and optimism.

Develop Healthy Self-Esteem

Self-esteem is more than just how we feel about ourselves. Self-esteem directly impacts how we show up in our relationships, our jobs, and our day-to-day lives. In essence, self-esteem is a confidence in one's own ability and worth. As author Jack Canfield said, "Self-esteem is made up primarily of two things: feeling lovable and feeling capable." Thankfully, a person's self-esteem is not fixed in place once he or she becomes an adult. It is fluid, rising or lowering along with various life events and experiences. Developing healthy self-esteem can improve your existing relationships and help you form new ones too.

SELF-ESTEEM IS A CONFIDENCE IN ONE'S OWN ABILITY AND WORTH.

- **Know the past is the past and the present is the present.** Recognize that to be emotionally healthy you must move from victim to victor. The strong person with a growing self-esteem is the one who refuses to let toxic past relationships control what happens in their relationships now.

- **Look for reasons to encourage others and believe in their ability to make decisions.** We can help those we love by supporting and encouraging them to use their gifts. People who have healthy self-esteem themselves are better able to respect and appreciate the abilities and skills of others.

- **Speak the truth as you see it, without fear of rejection and with no intent to harm others.** Speaking the truth lovingly is not dependent on whether the recipient is able to hear it. It is never part of our life's assignment to mind other people's business.

- **Separate feelings from the message being delivered.** Those with good levels of self-appreciation will find it progressively easier to separate emotions from the content of another's communication and will recognize the importance of differentiating between the two in their own communications.

- **Recognize the role that emotions such as anger, fear, and guilt play in people's lives.** Don't take these emotions at face value, but instead learn to look beneath the surface to determine the reason for and source of those emotions.

- **Live with an attitude of humility.** When others discover our gifts and talents, our self-esteem immediately feels the positive thrust of that affirmation.

Identify *and* Develop Your Gifts

You are not flawed just because a significant person in your past said you were defective. It doesn't matter if that individual was a parent, teacher, church leader, or coach. Because you were impressionable, you believed the negative messages heaped on you.

Right now you must ask yourself, *Who holds the power over my life today?* The answer is not any of those shaming people; it's the person you see in the mirror.

An ideal place to start in overcoming shame is identifying the gifts God has endowed you with—gifts you might not even be aware of currently. You may not recognize your gifts because your energy has been diverted to defensive coping mechanisms or because no one has affirmed your innate talents. Shame-filled people often overlook their own gifts or diminish them. That's

> "WHAT IS THE PRICE OF TWO SPARROWS—ONE COPPER COIN? BUT NOT A SINGLE SPARROW CAN FALL TO THE GROUND WITHOUT YOUR FATHER KNOWING IT. AND THE VERY HAIRS ON YOUR HEAD ARE ALL NUMBERED. SO DON'T BE AFRAID; YOU ARE MORE VALUABLE TO GOD THAN A WHOLE FLOCK OF SPARROWS."
> —Matthew 10:29-31 NLT

tragic because each person on earth—including you—is uniquely gifted to enrich and bless the world in specific ways.

To explore your unique areas of giftedness, finish these sentences:

- The subject that came the easiest to me in school was _____.

- I feel passionate about _____.

- I never feel more energized than when I _____.

- Ever since I was young, I've always loved to _____.

As you begin to recognize and use your gifts, you will develop a better self-image, higher energy, and stronger confidence. Part of developing healthy self-esteem is making a commitment to yourself to develop your personal strengths—not to impress others, but for your own sake and in service to God. If you wish to live out your giftedness and heal from shame, then it's critical that you invest the time and energy to enhance your gifts. And then look for ways you can serve others and make the world a better place.

CONQUER SELF-CONSCIOUSNESS

Nearly everyone feels self-conscious at times: on a first date, at a job interview, while giving a presentation. That's natural. But those who feel weighed down by shame often feel heightened self-consciousness, acutely aware of how they come across to others and how they are received. To ease feelings of awkwardness and discomfort:

Focus on one of your wonderful qualities.

Sure, you have some weaknesses—which are outweighed by your strengths. Pick one of the favorite things about yourself and dwell on it for a while.

Be okay with being you.

You're a unique combination of qualities, experiences, and beliefs—and there's no need to try to be like anyone else. Your social anxiety will evaporate when you realize you can simply be you.

Push yourself to participate.

Self-consciousness can lead you to be a wallflower, staying quiet in groups of people and wanting to hide. Let intentional involvement triumph over your anxieties.

Do your best—and let go of the rest.

In any situation—on a date, at work, in sports—your only goal should be to do your best. Self-consciousness will lose its grip when you know you've given your all.

Expect to be liked.

The principle of the self-fulfilling prophecy says that what you anticipate usually happens. Despite your awkward feelings, believe that you are indeed admirable and likable and then your personality and behavior will reflect that.

Know your true value.

Self-consciousness will diminish when you understand that your real worth is based on internal qualities, not external ones.

Improve what you can.

You might be self-conscious about a particular trait you consider a flaw. If so, do what you can to create improvement.

Accept what you can't improve.

Accepting ourselves doesn't come naturally for most of us, but it's essential for conquering self-consciousness. If you struggle with self-acceptance, it's important to remind yourself that no matter what misperceptions you have about yourself, the truth is, if you've put your faith in Jesus, then God finds you forever accepted in him! As Jesus said, "All those the Father give me will come to me, and whoever comes to me I will never drive away" (John 6:37).

Reclaim *Your* Personal Power

If you've suffered from shaming, you may doubt your ability to make good decisions. Reclaiming your personal power means learning to love and trust yourself. For instance, a man I worked with went back to school and began a second career, realizing his first career had been his father's decision, not his own. A woman I worked with started parenting her young kids according to her own convictions, instead of always following her mother's advice. I've seen people pursue new goals, relocate to a new town, and join a new church as declarations of independence and reconnection with their personal power. In each case they battled fear, yet they experienced exhilaration at connecting with themselves instead of trying to be or please someone else.

> "WISE CHOICES WILL WATCH OVER YOU. UNDERSTANDING WILL KEEP YOU SAFE."
> —Proverbs 2:11 NLT

To move forward in your effort to reclaim your personal power, start with these strategies:

- **Recognize that you are responsible for your own choices and actions.** As the apostle Paul tells us, "Each one should test their own actions. Then they can take pride in themselves alone, without comparing themselves to someone else, for each one should carry their own load" (Galatians 6:4–5).

- **Understand that you "teach" people how to treat you.** All your communication, verbal and nonverbal, accrues to show another person how you expect to be treated. This applies to family relationships, friendships, dating, work, and every other context. Refuse to put up with mistreatment of any kind; expect to be treated with respect and dignity.

- **Speak, don't smolder.** If you feel that someone is trying to take advantage of you or disregard your wishes, you might be tempted to silently fume and seethe. Remaining silent might avoid conflict but won't resolve anything—or show respect for yourself. If you feel you're being disrespected or disregarded, say exactly what you believe is happening. This will demonstrate that you have a backbone and give the other person a chance to explain.

- **Don't allow others to control your emotions.** Powerful personalities in your life may try to make you feel bad, guilty, or inferior. But you—and you alone— are in charge of your feelings and convictions. Therefore, you must be your own advocate. Your value as an individual is not determined by anything someone else does to you or says about you.

■ **Resist the temptation to apologize for your thoughts or feelings.** It's always helpful to say you're sorry if you've done something wrong, but feeling a certain way isn't wrong and doesn't warrant an apology. When called for, offer a firm but polite assertion or rebuttal. You can say, "I need to tell you that I take offense at your comment." Or, "I believe what you did is unfair. Let me tell you why."

Safeguard Yourself *with* Sturdy Boundaries

Being shamed is a form of emotional abuse designed to convince you through words and actions that you are powerless and without value. *This is a lie.*

You do indeed have power and value. You have the right not to be shamed by others. You have the power to say no if someone intends to hurt you. You have the choice to move on with your life free from damaging relationships. Bottom line: You have the right to set sturdy boundaries.

Boundaries don't have to be unfriendly, but they are necessary. One benefit is that they can help keep toxic people away from the passionate life you want to live. The less you allow an invasion of heart-snatchers, the less poison you will take into your own system. Mentally, put up a "boundary crossing" sign to help remind you where people may have overstepped their privileges in the past—and may continue to do so in the present. These instances of overstepping may be well-meaning but are negative influences. They may come in the form of emotional abuse that you've allowed to rule your life, making you feel inadequate and inferior.

YOU HAVE THE RIGHT NOT TO BE SHAMED BY OTHERS.

If you're seeking freedom from shame, the last thing you need are people who drag you down and convey the message that you don't measure up. Boundaries protect you from those who want to control and criticize you.

Knowing your limits is great, but only if you can effectively let others know as well. It is surprisingly difficult for many people to verbalize what they want and need. I'd like to share some tips for making that easier:

1. **Keep it simple.** Make the effort to boil down the key points of your boundaries to a single sentence or phrase. This helps you crystalize and clarify what you want in precise terms—and makes it easier for others to digest it as well. Try creating two

bulleted lists—one for the items you "must have" in your life and relationships; and another for those things that you "will not tolerate." For example: "I must know that my feelings matter" and "I will not tolerate shaming behavior of any kind."

I must have ...

- _____
- _____
- _____
- _____
- _____

I will not tolerate ...

- _____
- _____
- _____
- _____
- _____

2. **Write it down.** Part of the problem with tough conversations is that few of us are skilled at thinking on our feet. The message we want to communicate sounds great in our heads, but as soon as we start speaking, the words get tangled. One unexpected question from the other person is enough to derail the train entirely. Making a list of talking points in advance, when you can choose your words carefully and be precise with what you mean, will help keep your feet under you.

3. **Choose the right time.** If either of you is tired, rushed, or stressed by other things, that's not the right time for a discussion. Do what you must to be sure you are both at your best to have a productive conversation.

4. **Set the stage.** Difficult discussions sometimes get off on the wrong foot because the other person feels taken off guard. Avoid this by scheduling a time to talk and letting the person know in advance what you want to discuss. This communicates that you consider the conversation to be much more than casual—and gives the other person the chance to mentally prepare.

5. **Stay calm.** If you've done the work of defining your boundaries in the previous step, then there

is nothing for you to defend or justify. You are simply stating what is true for you, with no need for anyone else's approval or consent. With this in mind, you can focus on keeping your cool if the other person grows tense.

6. **Enforce your boundaries.** Your boundaries mean very little unless they are followed through on. You know what you want and need. You've let the other person know as well. Now comes the challenging part: ensuring those boundaries are respected and enforced. Making sure those rules are followed is key to preventing future harm.

   - *Be consistent.* Once you've communicated your boundaries, then it's up to you to avoid letting things slide. Mixed messages will undermine everything you've worked toward.

   - *Be firm.* People often fail to consistently enforce their own boundaries because they fail to understand the difference between assertiveness and aggression. We fear appearing pushy or combative. But clear, direct communication is perfectly reasonable behavior—and necessary when it comes to holding your ground.

   - *Be grateful.* Don't be afraid to acknowledge when someone succeeds in changing their behavior to accommodate your boundaries. This shows that you value their effort, and it reinforces respect for one another.

Deal *with* Offenses *in a* Healthy Way

People struggling with shame and seeking to overcome it are sometimes unsure how to deal with offenses that come up in everyday life. When someone offends them with insensitive words or deeds, they tend to have a pendulum swing of reactions, either responding by overreacting with aggression (as discussed in the previous chapter) or by withdrawing into themselves, feeling hurt and refusing further vulnerability.

Since contentious interactions are part of life and part of every relationship, it's important to handle them effectively and efficiently. I've found the following actions helpful in dealing with offenses:

- **Place the offense in the present, not in the past.**
  A harsh comment by a coworker today is not a validation of harsh comments experienced in your past. That coworker doesn't know about your past and is not intentionally trying to add to it. Maybe he had a bad day or is worried about something that has nothing to do with you. Learn to separate what is happening now from what happened then.

- **Give up the need to be right.** This is a hard one, but other people are entitled to their own thoughts and opinions. You might view something they did as hurtful, but they might not. When differences of opinion arise, recognize that sometimes the most you can achieve is the ability to respectfully disagree.

- **Take responsibility for yourself.** You are in charge of your own thoughts and actions. Avoid the temptation to blame others for "making" you do something. Moving past shame involves the power to make your own decision, even your own mistakes.

- **Respond instead of react.** Shame may have made you extremely sensitive to offenses by others and quick to respond with knee-jerk reactions. If you feel yourself immediately reacting, slow down, take a deep breath, say a prayer, and ask for a moment to collect your thoughts. Think before you act; that is the essence of intentional response.

- **Try to build a bridge, not burn one.** Even though you may be hurt or dismayed by what the other person said or did, you can still respond politely and respectfully. This way, you will be able to gauge whether what you experienced was a mistake or a misunderstanding. Be open to the possibility you misconstrued their words or deeds and seek to clarify intent.

- **Recognize the difference between the target and the source.** Some angry people spread their anger onto everyone and everything they can find. You may be the target of that anger, but you are not the source. Shame can cause you to take on undeserved responsibility. Be alert to accepting false guilt from others.

- **Retain your personal happiness.** You are in charge of your own attitude and response. If the hurt another person caused was unintentional, this can serve as a reminder that people make mistakes, including yourself. If the hurt was intentional, you can be alert to future dealings with this person. Either way, why hang on to the hurt? Fretting about it and replaying it in your mind will only hurt you again. Don't use someone else's hurtful action to bash yourself.

■ ■ ■

After that summer at Victory Cove Camp, I returned home riding high. I entered my senior year with renewed energy, motivation, and focus. By the end of the school year, I surprised myself again by finishing first in my class. In one year, I went from near the bottom of my class to first.

That week at camp was a turning point for me. I learned some valuable lessons through that experience. I learned that I could take risks. I learned that I could trust myself to accomplish more than I ever thought I could. I learned that, although there are people in this world who leave us with wounds of shame, there are also good people like John who believed in me and who want to do good unto others. And when we let those trustworthy, caring people into our lives, they will help us take another step toward freedom from shame.

CHAPTER 4

Achieving Lasting Freedom *from* Shame

Julie remembered with vivid clarity the day she became her mother.

Up to that time, she'd made it a point to act differently from her mother—to live a better life and never give her mother an excuse for her bad behavior. Growing up, Julie endured an endless stream of harsh remarks and stinging criticism. When her mother drank too much or was under stress or just in a foul mood, she would spit cruel words at Julie:

- "You're a sponge! All you do is drain my energy and my money."

- "I wouldn't get so upset if you were more help around the house."

■ "I should've listened to my mother and put you up for adoption."

Her mother had an equally inexhaustible supply of excuses for her own behavior: the world was against her, and Julie was supposed to understand when her mother was short-tempered, moody, cynical, and preoccupied. Julie learned to say nothing, to make no protests on her own behalf, and to swallow her anger and bow her head against her mother's rage. It was the only way to survive.

Survival meant staying underneath her mother's radar. And as long as her rage was directed at something or someone else, Julie was safe. But inside, she vibrated with a rage of her own that manifested itself in a cold and distant relationship with her mother.

As the years passed, Julie did not—would not—forgive her mother.

Then it happened. Julie's daughter, who had been potty training for the previous week, had an accident. Well, not an accident really. Julie was sure that her daughter, McKenna, knew she needed to use the bathroom but chose to stay seated on the couch so she could finish watching cartoons.

It didn't matter that McKenna wasn't yet two years old. All that mattered was a stressful day, soiled pants, and a stained couch. Before Julie knew what she was doing, she yelled at her daughter, "You miserable child! This is the thanks I get for all I do for you!" Then she jerked McKenna up from the couch and set her roughly on the toilet. There was no denying her displeasure, and McKenna responded by crying at the top of her lungs.

Julie looked at her daughter and felt satisfaction at her distress. "That's right. You should feel bad," Julie thought. "You deserve it."

And in that moment, she became her mother.

Thankfully, the story did not continue on this same trajectory year after year, as it had with Julie. Later that night as she lay awake in bed, Julie realized to her horror that she was capable of treating her own daughter the same way she'd been treated. The revelation made her sick to her stomach.

This episode, when Julie's anger caused her to shame her daughter, was a wake-up call and prompted her to seek help in therapy. When she came to The Center: A Place of Hope, she began working through her pent-up anger and deep-down shame. My team and I walked her through the steps toward healing from shame.

■ ■ ■

Seek Moments *of* Stillness *with* God

To combat shame, we need to slow down and seek moments of stillness so we can receive healing from our heavenly Father. But for people struggling with shame, this can be a very uncomfortable thing to do.

YOU CAN BEGIN TO HAVE A NEW RELATIONSHIP WITH GOD FOR WHO HE REALLY IS.

In my counseling practice, one of the most significant issues I encounter in my clients' lives has to do with their view of God. In most cases where people have a distorted view of God, the root issue lies with the relationship they have (or had) with their earthly father (and to a lesser degree, with their mother). In other words, the way in which we view our earthly father is embedded in us. When these impressions become baked into our heart, it is difficult to undo or correct the issue in our head. If our father was emotionally or physically abusive when we were very young, we may get the message, "Dads (or men) are not to be trusted."

Sure, as we grow up and mature, we can tell ourselves that only some men can't be trusted, and that most men are okay people. But that lie still whispers the message,

"Don't trust God because he's a father, and fathers can't be trusted."

Your earliest memories of your own father—as good or bad as he might have been—can be recognized by your adult self for exactly what they are: memories, not current realities that continue to distort your image of God. You can begin to have a new relationship with God for who he really is: Your heavenly Father who loves you completely and unconditionally.

Remember what I said earlier about replacing the script of shame? Look at what the Bible says about who God is and how he sees you, and overwrite shame's message with this truth:

- "The LORD does not look at the things people look at. People look at the outward appearance, but the LORD looks at the heart" (1 Samuel 16:7).

- "I no longer call you servants, because a servant does not know his master's business. Instead, I have called you friends, for everything that I learned from my Father I have made known to you" (John 15:15).

- "God demonstrates his own love for us in this: While we were still sinners, Christ died for us" (Romans 5:8).

How can we "be still and know that he is God" (Psalm 46:10)? To truly quiet our inner self, a few things need to occur:

1. **We need to retreat from the distractions of the world.**

2. **We need to make a conscious effort to calm our minds and listen to God.**

3. **We must face our present realities, both internally and externally.**

This three-step process is difficult; it takes energy and commitment, and it means we need to come to terms with ourselves. It means being fully honest and facing the pain of any discomforting or negative emotions and thoughts. It means turning off the noises and clutter in our brains and listening.

> "IN HIM AND THROUGH FAITH IN HIM WE MAY APPROACH GOD WITH FREEDOM AND CONFIDENCE."
>
> –Ephesians 3:12

There are myriad ways to get quiet and allow God to speak to you. One of the simplest ways to do this is to go somewhere safe and quiet where you feel relaxed. If, when you try to quiet your mind, you are inundated with every item on your mental to-do list, keep a pad of paper and pen next to you and write down those items to be dealt with later.

Then, once you are truly in a peaceful place, allow God to attend to your hurts, negative emotions, and self-doubt.

The first time (or first few times) you try this quieting exercise, you may find it difficult. It's hard for me to sit quietly and attune my ear to hear God. But like any other spiritual discipline, with time you will be able to enter more deeply into his peace and presence.

Grant Forgiveness—*for* Your Own Health

When you begin to explore your shame and its roots, you will likely find yourself becoming angry and embittered toward the source—the person—who planted and cultivated the seeds of that damaging emotion. This is especially true with unhealthy parents who damaged you over many years, and experiences of trauma, where someone devastated you through physical, sexual, emotional, or spiritual abuse.

FORGIVENESS IS ABOUT GIVING UP THE NEED TO BE RIGHT AND SETTING YOURSELF FREE!

What can you do with your justified and natural bitterness?

Forgive.

People who seek our help at The Center are often surprised when we ask about broken or embittered relationships in their lives. They fail to see the link between their emotional distress and unresolved conflict with others. But our experience has removed all doubt that hanging on to offenses and emotional wounds is an effective way to punish yourself. As the adage goes, "Before you embark on a journey of revenge, dig two graves."

The sticking point for most people is a burning desire for justice. They can't bear to let someone "get away with" some hurtful offense. But letting someone off the hook is not the essence of forgiveness at all. Rather, it's about your own experience of life's inevitable conflicts and whether you want to go on reliving that pain or let go and move on.

> "BE KIND AND COMPASSIONATE TO ONE ANOTHER, FORGIVING EACH OTHER, JUST AS IN CHRIST GOD FORGAVE YOU."
>
> —Ephesians 4:32

Here's a mental picture I came across years ago and have reminded myself of many times when it's my turn to forgive. In the South, children catch crawfish from the creek by baiting a paperclip on a string with a morsel of bacon. The poor creature clamps on and won't let go, even when hauled out of the water to its doom. That's precisely what happens when people refuse to forgive. After all, forgiveness is about giving up the need to be right and setting yourself free!

Beyond the personal benefits of forgiveness, however, lies something deeper—something that opens the door to transformative living. Forgiveness is a mental and spiritual posture that invites healing. Forgiving those who've harmed us is a way of acknowledging and accepting that we're all in need of mercy and compassion from God and from each other.

Because the process of forgiveness is so often confusing and misunderstood, I want to offer several thoughts for you to ponder today:

- To forgive and let go is not a matter of letting someone off the hook for hurtful behavior; it is an intentional decision to no longer be anchored to the past.

- To forgive and let go is not to try to change or blame another but to make the most of myself and recognize God's design for my life.

- To forgive and let go does not mean I stop caring; it does mean I will no longer take responsibility for the actions of others.

- To forgive and let go is to no longer judge but allow another to be a human being.

- To forgive and let go is to no longer deny but accept.

- To forgive and let go is to no longer regret the past but grow and live for today and the future, using experiences as opportunities for growth.

I invite you to add your own thoughts about what forgiveness means to you as you take steps to overcome shame.

To me, forgiveness means ...

- _____

- _____

- _____

- _____

- _____

Accept (*and* Extend) God's Grace

Sometimes our own power isn't enough to move what's blocking us, like seeking to overcome the daunting emotion of shame. It's like trying to push an eighteen-wheeler off the road by yourself. Impossible!

Much of the pain in our lives is a consequence of the actions of others wounding us, and our own harmful choices compound the pain. To heal, we must learn to differentiate between the two.

> "NOW THE LORD IS THE SPIRIT, AND WHERE THE SPIRIT OF THE LORD IS, THERE IS FREEDOM."
>
> –2 Corinthians 3:17

But it's not enough to stop there; we must take the next step and accept what these wrong actions have done to our lives. And I believe the only way to accept this difficult truth is by saying *yes* to God's grace in our own lives and extending that grace to others. When we are stuck in shame and can't forgive ourselves for past actions, we can't easily operate in grace and acceptance. After all, if we can't accept ourselves for who we are, how can we be expected to accept others? As with shame in every aspect of our lives, it's an inside-out job. We must come to the end of ourselves—our own attempts to quell and conquer the shame—and receive God's grace. When we accept forgiveness in exchange for our shame, we have a much greater capacity to accept others at face value.

As with love and forgiveness, the concept of grace goes against our very nature. Grace is freely given and cannot be earned; it's extended to those who don't deserve it. Although grace is hard to understand, God means for us to have it and experience it. I've heard grace defined as unmerited favor. If you don't have to do anything to earn it, then it's free. But you could ask, *If it's free, how is it worth anything?* You might be on the right track—if grace were free. But it isn't. You and I receive forgiveness at no cost, but it came at a tremendous price to Jesus, who paid with his life on the cross. As the apostle Paul said, "For you know the grace of our Lord Jesus Christ, that though he was rich, yet for your sake he became poor, so that you through his poverty might become rich" (2 Corinthians 8:9).

> **WHEN WE ACCEPT FORGIVENESS IN EXCHANGE FOR OUR SHAME, WE HAVE A MUCH GREATER CAPACITY TO ACCEPT OTHERS AT FACE VALUE.**

When we are staring at that huge, eighteen-wheel truck of a problem or trauma blocking our path, God's grace is the powerful machine that pushes that obstacle out of the way. We aren't powerful enough to do it, but God is. An acceptance of God's grace allows you to put the past behind you.

But grace is much more than just erasing the past; it is about writing the future. That's because freedom from the thicket of regret, blame, and shame enables us to show grace to others in every situation. It's the ultimate form of paying it forward.

So, is God asking us to "act" as though we're whole and perfect, as if our wounds never happened? Certainly not. It's about inviting him into the wound. As the Great Physician, he wants to apply his healing to your heart and mind.

GRACE IS MUCH MORE THAN JUST ERASING THE PAST; IT IS ABOUT WRITING THE FUTURE.

Spiritual acceptance is a trust process. But when you do surrender your past and give God your wounds, he will be faithful to bring you on a journey of restoration. Along the way, his love will begin to replace the pain in your heart— so much so that you will have an excess, and that extra love will spill out of your life and into the lives of others.

Find Support *with* Professional Guidance

Shame is such a deep-rooted issue that many people benefit tremendously from the guidance and insights of a qualified therapist or counselor. Your steps toward healing may need to take place (at least initially) with a professional who can assist you, providing a place of safety to explore the origins of your shame and tailor a plan for you to pursue wellness.

As you continue the journey to stability, it's crucial that you continue getting regular professional help through counseling, for as long as necessary. Talk therapies can be especially helpful. At The Center, we use a form of talk therapy called dialectical behavioral therapy, which is a clear and cogent process for working through strong emotions and shifting them from harmful to helpful. Using these techniques or others, a compassionate counselor can show you all the ways in which emotions have turned into maladapted behaviors—and equip you to exchange negative responses for constructive ones. With God's help and a counselor's encouragement, you can move forward on a healthy path.

A sign of emotional health is the willingness to access professional resources in times of need. Sometimes problems are so pressing that outside assistance is vital, and it's a sign of wisdom and courage to take advantage of it.

■ ■ ■

At the beginning of this chapter, I told you about Julie who painfully discovered that shame begets shame. That is, unless addressed and worked through, shame almost always gets passed along to others. That is not an inheritance we want to leave to our children. That is not a white elephant gift our friends like to receive. That is not a contribution our churches desire or need.

As for Julie, through her yearlong therapy process, she came to understand that her mother was a broken, bitter woman whose desperate, controlling need for love suffocated and shamed others, leaving little room to respond otherwise. Through a series of small steps, Julie forgave her mother. And with carefully considered boundaries in place, she began to restore a relationship with her mother. Most of all, she came to love herself in a healthy way and love her daughter with grace and tenderness.

The cycle of shame had been broken.

YOU CAN BE SET FREE!

Jesus says to you ...

"THE SPIRIT OF THE LORD IS ON ME,
BECAUSE HE HAS ANOINTED ME
TO PROCLAIM GOOD NEWS TO THE POOR.
HE HAS SENT ME TO PROCLAIM FREEDOM FOR THE PRISONERS
AND RECOVERY OF SIGHT FOR THE BLIND,
TO SET THE OPPRESSED FREE."
—Luke 4:18

The Secret Weapon *to* Defeat Shame

Mark's marriage ended badly. He fought tenaciously to keep the relationship intact, until his wife made it quite clear she no longer wanted anything to do with him. She was done with the marriage. It didn't matter how much he still loved her; she no longer loved him. She couldn't even stand to be anywhere near him.

She'd found someone else, and she wanted that relationship more than she wanted him. She was finished—and for a time, Mark thought he was too. Nothing made sense anymore. He couldn't understand what he'd done wrong or why someone who had loved him once could come to hate him so much. Had she ever really loved him at all? How could he have been so blind?

Mark felt ashamed. For not seeing the unraveling relationship for what it was. For believing he'd let down many people, including his parents, strong believers in the sanctity of marriage. For being duped—and dumped.

For a long time after the divorce, he didn't want to see anyone. His friends had been their friends, and some were now only her friends. With a morbid fascination, he tried to keep up with what she was doing, checking her social media pages daily. That ended when he discovered she had remarried. She was moving on with her life, and Mark couldn't seem to get on with his. What right did she have to be happy when she'd made him absolutely miserable?

A good friend finally took him aside and told him it was time to let his ex-wife go. During the time they were married, he had held onto her out of love. After the divorce, Mark had held onto her out of anger. He needed to let her go—to let the anger go. It was like a breath of air sweeping over his heart when he found the strength to forgive her and move on. He decided he was not going to concentrate on those last ten months but on the five years before that when he'd been happy.

Mark realized he was grateful to her for helping him develop an understanding of love. Ultimately, she threw it away, but Mark found he was ready to reclaim it. With his renewed confidence in his ability to give and receive love, Mark was ready to put the past behind him and embrace the future, with joy and without shame.

Gratitude Strengthens Hope

What is the antidote for every toxic thing that comes into our lives?

I believe it's *gratitude*.

Gratitude fosters optimism, which strengthens hope. That's why it's hard to imagine more effective soul medicine than gratitude. The list of things we can and should be thankful for—even in our darkest moments—is practically inexhaustible.

Granted, sometimes your troubles make it hard to muster gratitude for the big things like being alive or the loved ones in your life. So start with the little things in life. Try saying thanks for your favorite movie, crisp leaves on a fall day, the taste of your favorite tea, the phone call from your best friend, the sound of a giggling child, or the chance to sleep in on a Saturday morning. Being grateful for the small things will start to change your perspective and you will soon be able to see how precious each gift in your life is.

The physical and mental health benefits of gratitude have been well chronicled. For example, researchers at Harvard University conducted an analysis of numerous studies and concluded:

> In positive psychology research, gratitude is strongly and consistently associated with greater happiness. Gratitude helps people feel more positive emotions, relish good experiences, improve their health, deal with adversity, and build strong relationships.[9]

Gratitude Grows

Gratitude has a way of spreading exponentially—the more you choose to be grateful, the more you will find to be grateful for. You will notice the beauty all around us in the world, and you will have acute awareness of the loving God responsible for it all. When dark thoughts threaten to push everything else aside, purposeful gratitude to our Creator is a powerful way to push back.

I love the words of the medieval theologian Meister Eckhart who said, "If the only prayer you ever say in your entire life is thank you, it will be enough." By *enough*, I think he meant that gratitude is a sign of spiritual maturity. People who recognize their blessings and give thanks for them are living the essence of happiness, health, and healing.

It may seem impossible to be grateful for the shame you feel. And it's true that shame was not a "gift" you asked for or wanted. Still, the experiences that brought you shame have shaped who you are today, and it's your choice to take something negative and find something positive out of it, allowing it to make you stronger. If there has been a theme running through these pages, it is this: You are enough, you are accepted, you are loved *deeply* by your Creator. And as you take steps to find freedom from shame, you'll continue growing and reaching your full potential.

That is a reason for gratitude!

Notes

1 Mary Lamia, "Shame: A Concealed, Contagious, and Dangerous Emotion," *Psychology Today* (April 4, 2011).

2 Author unattributed, "Understanding Organizational Culture," *Principles of Management*, University of Minnesota Libraries Publishing edition (2015).

3 Oxford English Dictionary Online (accessed March 1, 2022).

4 "Fat Shaming and Body Shaming," Bully Statistics. *http://www.bullyingstatistics.org/content/fat-shaming-and-body-shaming.html.*

5 "Fat Shaming and Body Shaming."

6 "11 Facts About Body Image," DoSomething.org. *https://www.dosomething.org/us/facts/11-facts-about-body-image.*

7   "Fat Shaming and Body Shaming."

8   "Public Health Implications of Excessive Use of
    the Internet, Computers, Smartphones and Similar
    Electronic Devices," World Health Organization
    (August 27–29, 2014).

9   "Giving Thanks Can Make You Happier," *Harvard
    Health Publishing* (August 14, 2021).

Image Credits

Images used under license from Shutterstock.com: ANDRIY B, Baimieng, and Natalia Baran cover, p. 3, 5, 11, 39, 61, 85, 103, 109; pathdoc p. 6; Carlos Amarillo p. 15; Photographee.eu p. 17; Suzanne Tucker p. 18; Rawpixel.com p. 19; tadamichi p. 21; atewi p. 25; Sasun Bughdaryan p. 28; Billion Photos p. 31; 13_Phunkod p. 32; Photobank.kiev.ua p. 34; KieferPix p. 40; Arturs Budkevics p. 42; Ariya J p. 43; Axel Bueckert p. 47; Lightspring p. 50; Dilok Klaisataporn p. 56; siam.pukkato p. 57; Purino p. 66; Evgeny Atamanenko p. 67; 9nong p. 76; Robsonphoto p. 80; Khorzhevska p. 88; Microgen p. 91; Konontsev Artem p. 92; Cristina Conti p. 95; Freshstockplace p. 97; peterschreiber.media p. 98; Andrey_Popov p. 105.

MORE RESOURCES FROM
DR. GREGORY L. JANTZ

Unmasking Emotional Abuse

Six Steps to Reduce Stress

Ten Tips for Parenting
the Smartphone Generation

Five Keys to Dealing
with Depression

Seven Answers for Anxiety

Five Keys to Raising Boys

Freedom From Shame

Five Keys to Health
and Healing

40 Answers for
Teens' Top Questions

When a Loved One Is Addicted

Social Media and Depression

Rebuilding Trust after Betrayal

How to Deal with Toxic People

The Power of Connection

www.hendricksonrose.com